for the

Golden Years

FROM JESUS WITH LOVE

Edited by Maria Fontaine

Cover by Doug Calder

ISBN 13: 978-3-03730-085-5

© 2008 Aurora Production AG, Switzerland

Printed in China

www.auroraproduction.com

DISTRIBUTORS

USA
Activated Ministries
PO Box 462805
Escondido, CA 92046–2805
Tel: 760 739 1240
E-mail: sales@actmin.org
www.activatedonline.com

Europe
Activated Europe
Bramingham Park Business Centre
Enterprise Way
Luton
LU3 4BU
United Kingdom
E-mail: orders@activatedeurope.com
www.activatedeurope.com

Canada
Coloring The World Productions
100 City Centre Dr. Box 2135
Mississauga, Ontario
L5B 3C7
Canada
E-mail: activatedcanada@ica.net

South Africa
Aurora Media
Suite 548
Private Bag X18
Lynnwood Ridge 0040
South Africa
Tel: 0861 105 898
Outside South Africa dial: +27 83 791 2804

INTRODUCTION

As we get older, so many of the things we experience are new to us—but they aren't new to Jesus. Throughout the ages He has been with those nearest and dearest to His heart during this stage of life, and He wants to extend that same personal tender loving care and attention to us. He knows the high points, the joys, and the fulfillment of a life well lived. He also knows our every pain, He sees our every tear, He understands our every fear and frustration, He sympathizes with us over every loss and disappointment, and He knows exactly what we need to enjoy life and come through every new challenge victoriously.

The following messages from Jesus are sure to provide encouragement and comfort when you need it most. And better still, they can help you open a personal hotline to Heaven through which you can receive the perfect answer to every question and need. Yes, you too can hear directly from Jesus. He will speak to anyone who believes in Him, sincerely asks Him to speak, and then accepts by faith that what they "hear" in their heart is truly His voice.

Open your heart to Jesus and receive His words of love and life. He can make these the best years of your life!

So much to give

*Y*our later years can be the ones of greatest fulfillment and greatest love. So many others can benefit from your wisdom, experience, and understanding of the true values of life. You see things more clearly now, for the frivolous cares of life have been replaced by a keener appreciation of the things that really matter.

This is something I want you to pass on to others, especially those who are struggling through the prime of life. While they may have energy, strength, ambition, and material success, almost without exception they don't have the wisdom and depth that you have. They couldn't possibly, because they haven't lived as much of life as you have.

The deeper things in life can only be gained through experience, which takes time. Open the storehouse of your heart and give to others from the treasures there.

The tapestry

Each event in a person's life, each thought, each decision, each bit of love, and each interaction with someone else is like a thread in a tapestry. Day after day, dark threads and bright threads are woven together, often, it seems, without rhyme or reason, but in the end they form a picture.

I'm looking at the tapestry of your life now, and it's beautiful! All the good things—the happiness and fulfillment, the love you gave and received, the lives that were better because of you—these are bright threads.

The dark threads are the difficulties and disappointments, the trials and the tears. These are also necessary because they make the bright threads look all the brighter and help give your tapestry its rich, warm glow.

No one else has ever woven a tapestry quite like yours, and no one could have. Your life is unique.

Forever young

A heart that's filled with love never grows old.

∽

Keep your heart filled with love—love for Me and love for others—and you will have found the fountain of youth.

∽

If some of your dreams are still before you, then you have not grown old.—You still have things to look forward to and to live for.

∽

As long as you are still learning, you are still living.

∽

It's better to be a hundred years young than forty years old.

∽

Age is a state of mind. If your heart and mind are young, *you* are young.

∽

Don't ever give up on living just because you can't do all that you used to. You wouldn't still be there if I didn't have something for you to do and didn't think you could do it. Find out what I have for you now, and put your heart into it.

Changing seasons

First you had your green years of springtime, when you were young and full of excitement and energy. Your days were filled with learning, experimenting, and finding your place in life.

Then came the growing, flowering years—the rich summer of your life, in which many of your earlier struggles paid off and dreams came to fruition.

Now you are in the autumn of your life, when the harvest is in and leaves turn from green to rich hues of red and gold.

At first this phase may seem like a letdown. You worry because you are losing abilities that you feel are necessary to lead a worthwhile and happy life. But if you can accept this season of life for the blessing I mean for it to be, you will still enjoy life to the full. You may not be able to do some of the things you used to, but this will give you more time for *better* things. It's all in how you view it. Sit back, relax, and enjoy the turning of the leaves. The many colored leaves that I bring out every fall show you the many aspects of the love and other blessings I have for you.

You are as a flower that is blooming late in life, with blossoms even more spectacular than the blooms that came out in early life. You are My masterpiece!

I will

When you are tired, I will be your resting place.
When you are in the dark, I will be your light.
When you are hungry, I will be your living bread.
When you are fearful, I will be your defense.
I will be all these things to you, because you are Mine.

When you are lonely, I will be your friend.
When you are in doubt, I will be your source of faith and courage.
When you are weary, I will be your strength.
When you are helpless, I will be your intercessor.
I will be all these things to you, because I love you so.

Nothing to offer?

Who says you have little or nothing to offer others? Everyone has needs, everyone has problems, and *you* just might be the one to fill someone's need or help solve their problem.

You could be the key that turns the lock so that I can set them free.

You could speak the word that lifts them from the depths.

You could smile and bring out the sun.

You could be just the medicine they need.

Your optimism could restore their will to live.

Your friendship could fill a vacancy in their life.

Your faith could spark their faith.

Your love could point them to My love.

You could be the answer to their prayer.

Earthen vessels

The Bible says, "We have this treasure in earthen vessels"—lowly clay pots—"that the excellence of the power may be of God and not of us" (2 Corinthians 4:7). That is the way I work. I use weak people, those who have no greatness or strength of their own, to show My power. That way there is no mistaking that those people are merely tools in My hand and that I am the One who deserves the credit for everything I do through them.

The way of the world is to be strong, self-reliant, and proud, but those who are truly great in My kingdom are those who walk the path of humility and dependence on Me. Choose this path and you can experience the best years of your life—years filled with love, joy, peace, patience, kindness, goodness, gentleness, and faith. All of these are fruits of My Spirit, which come from being close to Me.

The string of pearls

When a grain of sand finds its way into an oyster, it troubles the oyster at first. But the oyster covers the grain of sand with layer upon layer of nacre, until ever so slowly that grain of sand becomes a pearl.

In like manner, trials can be the source of beautiful "pearls" in your life. When you choose to accept them and trust Me to make the best of them, little by little over time, I cover over the prickly problem and make something lovely out of it.

Through difficulties I teach you things that you would never be able to learn so well any other way—patience, endurance, faith, optimism, and much more. Every time you trust Me and I bring you through a certain difficulty or phase of life, it brings forth another beautiful pearl. In the end, your life becomes like a full string of magnificent pearls.

Investing in the future

I've seen everything that you have ever done for others, and I haven't forgotten any of it. I am like a faithful accountant, and I make note of all these things in My book. Every kind word, every bit of love, and every unselfish deed is entered into My book. I also see every affliction, every hardship, every wrong you endure, and every trying of your faith. These are also recorded in My book.

In all of these things, you have been investing in eternity. You have given here and there, but you don't realize how much you have invested or how much interest your investment is earning for you. In the day of accounting, when I tally the books and you see how much you have stored up in the next life, you just might be surprised at the rewards that await you!

Lean on Me

I have fashioned you so you would feel the need to come to Me. If you did not have any difficulties, you would sail merrily along, content to have a peaceful, uneventful life. It is in your times of difficulty that you turn to Me, and find Me.

I will never give you more than you can bear. I am always here to hold and comfort you, because I love you. Put your full weight on Me, and let Me carry the worries, pains, and burdens, while you take a rest.

I will help you through each and every difficulty. You are never beyond My help, and nothing is too hard for Me. Come to Me, talk to Me, tell Me all your troubles, and let Me comfort and counsel you. In Me, you will find all you need.

Never alone

I've walked with you your whole life. I've been there at each turn. You haven't always felt My presence and you've sometimes wondered exactly where I was or if I was around at all, but no matter what you felt like or where you've been, I've always been near you. Sometimes I've even carried you. So what makes you think I'm going to stop caring for or being with you now? I'm as near as I've always been—just a whispered prayer away—and you are just as dear to Me.

All things work together for good in the lives of those who love Me. Please trust that everything I allow to come your way is for a good purpose—even things that don't seem very good at first. One day you will see the good in everything. I promise.

Cause and cure

*L*ife, as you know, is not all sunshine and gladness. You have had your share of difficulties, and many times you have felt that you were on your own. You have wondered why I let some things happen to you, so let Me explain.

Others were the cause of some of your problems. I could not always intervene in such cases because everyone has been given the majesty of choice. I'm sad that some people abuse that power and cause others to suffer. I am sorry that you have suffered because of others' wrong choices and lack of love.

Then I allowed other troubles, hoping that they would cause you to turn to Me and accept My help and love. You thought you could handle any difficulty and take care of yourself, but you couldn't. Sometimes you let Me help, and sometimes you didn't. But through it all, I never left you. Every time, I was there, waiting for you to ask.

Sometimes you hardened your heart in order to bear the pain and strain, and sometimes you blamed Me for your problems, as though I didn't love you. But I always have, and always will.

I'm still right beside you, wanting to be a part of your life. I can put your life back together if you will give Me all the pieces. I can answer your questions and ease your troubled mind. Talk to Me as a friend, as a brother, or however you want to picture Me. In the stillness of your heart I will whisper to you, and if you will listen with your heart, you will hear Me. Let Me prove Myself.

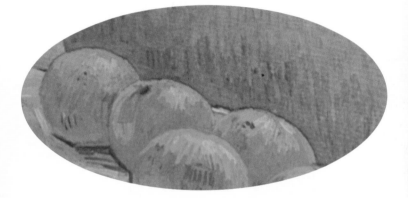

It's no accident when you feel
compassion for someone. It's My
heart touching yours with the
need to pray and help.

I forgive

Do not fear that I haven't forgiven you for some of the things you did wrong or the hurt you caused others. The moment you asked Me to wash away your sins and become your Savior, I forgave you not only for your past, but for your mistakes in the present and future as well. Nothing you have done or will do can ever take away your place in Heaven, nor will it take away My love for you.

You also don't need to worry that you will continue to suffer remorse over these things when you get to Heaven. In fact, you don't have to suffer remorse over them now. Just let them go! When I receive you, there will be only joy and rejoicing. I will be so happy to have you by My side.

❧

Don't waste a moment looking back. Remorse has no power to change the past. It only robs you of joy and kills your chances for present happiness and peace of mind.

Perfect peace

Every detail of your life and every concern of your heart, no matter how large or small, is important to Me. Trust each care to Me in prayer, and you'll find peace that fills your soul—peace such as you have never experienced before. Peace is the reward of faith and trust.

I have all the hairs of your head numbered.—That's how well I know you. If I've gone to the trouble to count your hairs, then don't you think I am concerned about the other, far more significant aspects of your life? I care about your happiness. I care about your health. I care about your financial situation. I care about your loved ones. I care about you, and if you trust Me, I will see to it that you always have what you need.

Rise above

*Y*ou're not coming to the end of your usefulness; you're just getting older. I know your body feels old, but your spirit doesn't have to be old.—It can be fresh and alive through the power of My Spirit. I can make life easier for you if you'll keep a positive attitude and draw your strength from Me.

Don't give in to feelings of depression and despondency. Don't languish in darkness and negativity. You can rise above all that on the wings of prayer. Turn your heart toward your destination—Heaven. Look forward in wonder at what is to come.

When hardships come your way, look on the bright side of things. Thank Me and praise Me for all the things I've done for you thus far. I've kept you through a lifetime of difficulties, and I'm not about to abandon you now.

What am I like?—I am the spirit of love itself. If you were to take the most loving thing that has ever happened to you and multiply that by a thousand, that would only begin to come close to understanding what I am like.

I love you for you

I love you—and not just for whatever good you have done and continue to do. I appreciate your labors of love and your loving prayers, because others benefit from them, but those good works don't earn My love. My love for you is a gift. I love you because you are you. It's as simple as that!

So stop thinking you have to accomplish great things to be great in My eyes or greatly loved by Me. You *are* greatly loved, and in My eyes, you *are* someone great! Just relax. Slow down, enjoy life, and enjoy Me most of all. Spend time with Me and you'll become more like Me. Then labors of love will follow so naturally that they won't seem like labors at all, but a joy.

ख

Each of My children is special to Me. I love each of you as if you were My only child.

This battle is Mine

Life is a battle, and like they say, it isn't over till it's over. Most of the troubles you experienced in your youth are behind you, but new troubles have taken their place.

When you were younger, it was at times easier for you to cope with troubles and come out on top. You were stronger and more resilient then. But now you're often finding that your own resources aren't enough.

It's time to change tactics. It's time to truly turn the fight over to Me. Each time you feel pain or discomfort, turn your heart toward Me in prayer. Each time you feel discouraged or frustrated, turn your thoughts into prayers. If you feel confused or fearful, put your hand in Mine. Give your cares to Me, and I will give you peace of mind.

ɞ

Your physical capabilities may be limited, but there is no limit to the spiritual power you can wield through prayer!

Forever friends

Some of the familiar faces that you spent many happy years with—some of your dearest friends—have gone on ahead of you to the next life. It's difficult not having them around anymore, I know. When you feel down because you miss them, think about how happy they must be now. They have left the cares and worries of life behind. They are in a better place, and they are looking forward to seeing you there when your time comes.

The happy memories of the good times you had together will live on forever. Each time you think about those dear ones that are no longer with you, you realize a little bit more how blessed you were to have known them and to have had their companionship. That closeness you shared was a gift from Me, and it's yours and theirs forever. When you come over to this side, you will be even closer and appreciate each other more than ever.

Closer than before

I do not separate loved ones through death. I have given you a spiritual link with your loved one. Even though he is no longer with you in body, you can still feel his presence and know that he is always with you in spirit. I will not leave you comfortless, and neither will he. He is even closer than before.

Through the years, you learned to almost read each other's mind. You knew what he was going to say or how he was going to react almost before he did, and vice versa. Now he *can* actually read your mind and, just as wonderful, you can hear his voice inside as he guides your thoughts and gives you reassurances of his forever love. This is My way of allowing you to continue to be together in spirit.

But that's not all. Your loved one also wants to help you learn to be more heavenly minded. He has already entered into the joys and rewards of Heaven, and he wants to share a little foretaste of that with you now.

So you see, your loved one's passing wasn't the end of your relationship, but the beginning of an even fuller and deeper one—a spiritual relationship.

I will wipe the tears from your
eyes on that day when we meet
face to face, and you will be
united again with those you love
who have gone on ahead of you.

ೞ

Before long, you and your
loved one will be together again
on this side of the veil—the veil
that now separates your world
from this heavenly one—and you
will live forever in the beautiful
home I have prepared for you.

Heavenly perspective

Your beloved who has left this life is safe in My arms, in her beautiful new home in Heaven. She is as happy and carefree as a little child because she is free from the pain that was wearing away her earthly body. She is young again—in the prime of life. I am sorry that you miss her so, but it was her time. She was ready and wanted to come to Me.

Now she understands what she could not understand before. She is blessed with more of My love and feels more secure in My love than ever before. She looks back on her life on earth and your time together, and sees only the good, just like I do. Won't you let Me give you the same heavenly perspective? Nothing would make her happier than to see you truly happy, with no regrets.

Loved by the light

If you have faith in Me, you have no need to fear the future. With Me in your heart, you can know that I will care for you all the days of your life and on into the next life. Find peace in knowing Me, believing in My love, and believing that there is a better world waiting.

Let the light of My love shine into your life. Find comfort and solace in this light. When you know that I love you, you can rest assured that everything is going to be okay.

I promised that I would not leave you comfortless, so My Spirit will be upon you in a special way. I will be closer to you and help fill all the empty places in your heart. Time spent with Me will refresh and encourage you, My dear friend.

No regrets

You have passed many of life's most difficult tests. You survived and even thrived through the things that came your way. Sometimes, though, you wonder if you have spent your life as wisely as you could have, and wish you had more to show for yourself. But I don't focus on your past. I look at what you can yet become, your present and future.

I want you to be happy, but first you must let go of your regrets and sorrow over the past. Don't fall into the trap of remorse, thinking that you failed or fell short and therefore don't deserve to be happy and fulfilled now or ever. That is not true!

I can help you make anything right, and you still have time to do so. Then you can look forward to a truly happy, fulfilling, and love-filled future, free of remorse and regrets. What could be more wonderful than that?

Let Me shine through you

Many Christians feel that they are supposed to be strong and always be "doing something" for Me, but their strength often gets in the way. When people are naturally strong, healthy, and gifted, others tend to focus on them. But when people are weak and afflicted, I have a chance to shine through. When all you have is Me, then you realize that I am enough. And when others see that all you have is Me, they realize that I am all they need. When you are weak, you are strong, because then My strength can be made perfect in your weakness.

Just tell yourself, "I'm weak and I'm sick and I can't do the things that I used to do, but the Lord is helping me through these afflictions. I've got His strength and His peace and His joy. I have faith for the future. I don't know about tomorrow, but I know the One who holds tomorrow in His hand. He's my friend, and I know He's going to care for me and bring me through whatever comes."

In this together

When I see you unhappy, it makes Me unhappy. When I see you struggle, I struggle with you. I know your heart and I feel your aches and pains. I am sorry that your aging body makes life difficult. I also know, though, that these ailments help bring about good in your spirit in the long run. Through them you become more understanding, more tolerant, and more sympathetic. When you have already experienced what others are going through, you can pull them up. You also feel moved to pray for them. Both encouraging others and praying for others bring blessings into your own life, as well as theirs.

I promise you that I will not let you suffer more than you are able to bear. I can soothe and minimize your pain. I will help you carry the weight of your afflictions. When we do it together, it won't be too heavy or too hard. When your weary body aches, turn to Me. Lean on Me. Focus your mind's eye on Me, and I will comfort and bring you through.

You are Mine, and I am yours—your ever-present, ever-faithful Savior and friend. I'm always here with you. I sit at your side to whisper sweet words that bring love and comfort and strength to your heart.

I'm right here. I'm not far off in Heaven somewhere, waiting for you to come to be with Me someday. I'm that friend that sticks closer than a brother. I gave My life for you, and I would gladly do it again, even if you were the only one. I love you that much, and you are that important to Me!

My Word, the Bible, is like a huge treasure chest, full of riches for you to discover. Ask Me to speak to you as you read it, and I will give you understanding and help you see how it applies to your life. It will be a source of wisdom that will both guide you and keep you. If you will fill your heart with good things from Me, you will receive more and more good things from Me.

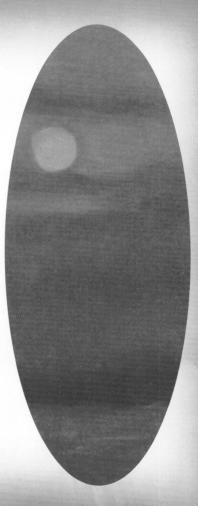

Listen and learn

I want to speak personally to you. I want to teach you to hear My voice so I can become even more a part of your life.

I want to guide you moment by moment. I want to show you how you can make the most of each day. I want to open your eyes to all the opportunities that lie before you. I want to show you how you can be an even bigger blessing to those around you and those dearest to your heart.

How will I do this? I will whisper to your heart whenever you open your spirit to Me. It's really very simple. The Bible says, "Ask and you will receive" (John 16:24), and that's the key to hearing from Me personally. Ask, listen, receive, and then believe.

No matter how old you are or how much you think you know, there is always more to learn and you can be learning something new every day. I can make each day a learning experience, a new discovery. I can answer all your questions and unlock the secrets of life—and it all begins with learning to hear from Me.

All part of the plan

I will not let anything happen to you that is not in some way part of My perfect plan for your life. Even times of illness are a part of My plan, because when you're alone with Me like this, I can comfort you, love you, and commune with you without other distractions. As you spend time praying and reading My Word, it can be a sweet time for both of us. I love to speak to your heart in the stillness. Rest in Me. Let Me love you, and let Me care for and comfort you.

☙

I love the way the rainbow shines in your heart after the rain of testing and difficulty. Your love for Me brings out the sunshine of My love and together we make dazzling colors.

Better the second time around

Some say that old age is like a second childhood, and in a way, that's true. It's a time to return to simple joys that were brushed aside in the rush to grow up, and then crowded out by the pressures of adult life. I said once that people must become like little children to enter the kingdom of Heaven, and that's really the way it works. As you get older, things become simple again. This simplicity brings you closer to Me and closer to Heaven.

Take advantage of this opportunity and enjoy your second childhood. No matter how old you are, you're still My child. Let Me prepare your heart for your journey home to Heaven, to that world where everything is beautiful and simple—simple discoveries, simple love, simple contentment, and simple joys.

Wanted: prayer warriors

The way the world is going, there is a greater need for prayer than ever before, yet My army of prayer warriors dwindles.

It is heartbreaking to see how many situations are not being helped because no one prays. I have power to do anything, but people's prayers are needed to activate the power.

Meanwhile, My lost children wander as sheep with no shepherd because no one pleads their case. Also, those who labor for Me could accomplish so much more with more prayer power behind them.

Will you become a prayer warrior? Will you pray fervently and consistently? There are thousands who you could help through prayer. Rise to the challenge, and you can help change someone's world. You may even help change the course of history from your humble corner. This ministry of prayer could be your crowning achievement.

Be open to love

It can be difficult to accept help, even when you're very weak or sick and know you need it. It can also be difficult to trust others. You may tend to think that you know what's best, and sometimes you do, but not always. You may be older and wiser in some ways, but it pays to listen to others.

Let your loved ones do what they can to make life easier for you. It's one way they have of showing their love. It is a touch of My love for you, too, when I put people in your life to help you. Accept their love, and accept My love.

Who's perfect?

on't feel bad about the mistakes you've made. Is there anyone who hasn't made a lot of mistakes? No. "All have sinned and fall short of the glory of God" (Romans 3:23), as the Bible says. But I don't look at your faults and failings. I look at the heart. Sure, there were things that you could have done better, but I don't condemn you. I see your love for Me. I see the good you have done. I see the love you gave to others. I see a heart that has been trying, in its own special way, to give what it could. To Me, that is the most beautiful thing there is.

 cз

I want to help you think about the wonderful times you've had and the wonderful times to come. If your hope is waning, I want to restore it. Won't you let Me?

Please pray!

- Pray for your loved ones, that their days will be full of love and meaning, and that I will become a real and important part of their lives.

- Pray for your friends. Commit their cares and problems to Me, and ask Me to help them.

- Pray for all the lost and lonely people of the world, that they will find Me, whom to know is life eternal.

- Pray for those with painful and debilitating ailments to find My healing, comfort, and strength.

- Pray for My workers who toil in the harvest fields to bring others to Me.

- Pray for world peace, and that the poor and oppressed will be liberated.

- Pray for the younger generation, into whose hands the world is passing.

- Pray for any others that you know need My love and help.

The golden treasure of time

Life is a treasure hunt. You sense this most as a child. A child's entire being is abuzz as he discovers the world around him. Life itself is one big surprise.

As time goes on, the treasures become fewer but more significant—a companion, a family, the realization of dreams and goals.

Then, just when you think the treasures have run out, there are more. One of the special treasures of old age is time. When you were young, time escaped you. But now there's more time to think. I made it this way so you could live closer to the Spirit of Heaven. Slow down and learn to enjoy the marvels of My creation and the workings of My Spirit.

The treasure of time can lead to so many other discoveries. Treasures everywhere! Gifts galore!

Career change

You don't need to retire from life; you just need a new career—and I've got the perfect one for you. What a wonderful counselor you would make!

You chuckle sometimes to see how worked up young folks get over things you learned to deal with ages ago. You've walked that path before and learned that things have a way of working out in the end, especially with prayer. At your age, you're not so intense about things. That's a valuable asset in such a busy world. The young often seek out the old for their wisdom, their perspective on life, and their approval and support. You can have a great effect on them.

Spending time with younger folks can also have a great effect on you. Their energy, enthusiasm, and passion for life will rub off and revitalize you. How's that for a perk?

Heritage of faith

I let you experience everything you have experienced in life for a purpose—and it has not only been for your own sake, but also for the sake of others. You have grown deeper in spirit because of your years of knowing Me. Now you need to pass on that faith to others. They need to see that faith really works, that prayer really works, and that I am real.

As you live your faith, it will have a great effect on others. Long after you're home in Heaven, your faith will carry on in others' lives. Your love for Me and My love for you will be reference points. You will be remembered as a person of faith, someone who loved and trusted Me and imparted a peaceful, gentle, loving spirit to everyone around you.

Be positive

You can't always choose your circumstances, but you can choose your outlook on life. You can choose to be stiff, stern, and grumpy, or to be upbeat, cheerful, and positive. Sure, you may sometimes feel down or you may be struggling with pain or discomfort, but that doesn't mean you can't be an encouragement to those around you.

Every stage of life has its upsides and its downsides. Focus on the upsides. Be positive. Think and talk about the good things—and keep at it for the rest of your days.

It says in the Bible that as a person thinks, so is he. If you make a habit of viewing situations positively, you will not only be happier for it, but you will be a positive person—the kind others love to be around.

Winning combination

You can't take your material possessions with you when you graduate to the next life, but you can take the wisdom and experience you've gained in this one. What you learned on earth will still be used in Heaven.

In Heaven you are finally going to be able to truly live life to the full. You will have a healthy body and be full of energy, like you were when you were young. On top of that, you'll have the wisdom you've gained over the years. That's quite the winning combination and something to look forward to, isn't it?

There will still be plenty to do in Heaven, too. You will have time to rest, relax, and absorb and enjoy the wonder of it all, but there will also be things to learn, places to discover, and exciting challenges. It won't be boring.—You can be sure of that!

Bringing out the sweetness

With each passing year, I see you become sweeter and sweeter. Through the years I've blessed you with more wisdom and more understanding of people and situations, and you've become more dependent on Me—the One who can guide you aright each step of the way. You're getting more and more radiant as you put your trust in Me.

Some people are afraid of the "golden years," but if they could only see the wonderful wisdom, experience, patience, and sweetness that only this phase of life can bring, they'd realize that this is a time to treasure.

ॐ

A fine wine improves with age. So it is with you, My special one. You are becoming better with age. Each year has added to your value, until now you are a prized vintage, smooth and mellow.

Let Me take the helm

Sometimes you feel like a small, aging boat. You would rather be tied up in dock than out in the deep where you are being battered and tossed by an angry sea. You're too old for all that, you say. But I am your captain, and you are in good hands. I know how to master the wind and waves, and I can guide you safely through the storms. I can even temper the wind and calm the waves for your sake.

Your heart is like the wheel. When you yield your heart to Me, I am able to steer the rest of you. Don't try to weather the storms on your own; call on Me for help. With Me at the helm you have nothing to fear. I'm perfectly able to bring you safely home again.

There is no need to fear the future or worry about the present. I am your Good Shepherd, and I will faithfully care for you. I know the way ahead. The path will never be too difficult if you stay close by My side and let Me lead you.

Let's talk about love

My love for you is unconditional. No matter how bad or unlovable you think you are, I still love you. I love you just because you are you. You are My creation. I know your weaknesses and I see every time you make a mistake or fall short, but that does not stop Me from loving you. When you are sorry and ask for My forgiveness, it makes Me love you even more.—And I am always ready to forgive.

❧

When you look into a child's smiling eyes, you're seeing a glimpse of Heaven. When you watch the sun setting peacefully on the horizon, you're seeing the reality of My loving presence. When a loved one reaches out a hand to help you, I'm reaching out through them to touch you with My love. There are so many ways you can see My love and loving ways, if you are looking.

My plans
for you are
perfect; My
love for you is
unending; My
grace for you is
sufficient.

Heaven's wonders

I know your heart's desires, I know what will make you happy, and I have prepared all those things for you here in Heaven. Whatever you want most is waiting for you here, and you'll be able to enjoy it to the full, forever. I have prepared for My loved ones exactly what I know will mean the most to each one. Heaven *is* all it's made out to be, and more. You will not be disappointed. Just wait and see!

All your dreams will come true. All your questions will be answered. All sadness will be gone forever. Anything you've ever wanted to learn about will be at your fingertips. Anything you've ever wanted to experience will be possible.—And that's not even the half of it!

 os

You are Mine forever, and I have a special place prepared for you with Me.

Sunrise

There is never a sunset without a sunrise—a glorious and splendid sunrise—and that is My promise to you in this life. Whenever a "sunset" comes your way, just remember I'll always bring a sunrise too. Whenever there is a low moment, a shadow that falls across your path, when disappointment darkens the way and the last glimmer of hope fades from sight, when the chill of the night closes in around you, just remember that the sunrise awaits you with all its life and light and glory and brilliance. And just as I have promised that the sun will rise every morning, so the sunrise of My love will light your life again.

No matter what sunsets you may encounter, I will always bring greater hope and happiness into your life. I will bring you through every night to the light of a better day.

The sanctuary

see your struggles and hear your calls for help. When you feel all alone, I am there. I feel your heartaches, and wait for you to come to Me in prayer. Come into My sanctuary, into that secret place that you and I can share. There I am able to lift the worries, the cares, and the confusion. There I can restore your feeling of purpose and infuse you with strength to go on.

Life can be a struggle, but you do not have to struggle alone. Many times I have placed burdens in your life that seemed like mountains. They weigh your spirit down and you wonder why I have placed them there. I have not done these things to reprove you or as some sort of punishment.—I have done them to bring you closer to Me. I know your heart better than anyone else ever could, and love you more dearly.

The problems and obstacles that I allow in your life can be taken two ways: They can make you either bitter or better. When you have found the peace that only I can give, I can then use you as an instrument of My love to comfort others.

Many things in life can seem unfair or even unloving, but when you look at them through My promise of "all things work together for good," that gives a whole new meaning to things. That promise holds the key to any heartache, any problem, or any fear.

I love you, My child, and I always will. You have a special place in My heart that no one else could ever fill.

You will come to this realm in My time, when your task on earth is finished. This is one of the special rewards that I give to those who love Me: You can know that I will bring you to Me at the perfect time—no sooner and no later.

A word of advice from the Great Physician

on't resist the changes that naturally take place at this time of life, but accept them and learn to enjoy your new lifestyle for what it is. Resisting only puts more strain on your health and happiness.

Stay active, but don't try to do more than you can. Don't push yourself too hard. Give yourself a break; let others do the heavy work. I know that is easier said than done when you're used to being independent and strong and active. It's hard to step back, but you have to at some point.

Try to get exercise in some form every day, preferably in the fresh air. Exercise will help you stay fit and sleep better, and will help you feel more energetic overall. Just the fact that you're being active has a good effect on you physically and mentally. It lifts your spirit and improves your general health. If you're not following My simple health guidelines or respecting the changing needs and limitations of your body, you can expect some trouble. But if you exercise, eat properly, get the sleep you need, and give your troubles to Me, you can trust Me to do the rest.

Out of touch?

on't worry about not being able to keep up with the latest technology or not understanding what drives the younger generation. There's no reason to feel out of touch or left behind, because if you're in touch with Me, you're in touch with what really counts. All the rest that people pursue in their quest for happiness and fulfillment in life is a sham. It may catch and hold their attention for a while, but when all is said and done, it will leave them as empty inside as they were before.

Nothing but My love can ever truly satisfy the heart. So if you have My love, you have what others need most and are searching for, even if they don't realize it.

ଓ

Your sweet company encourages many. Keep on giving out My love as you give cheer, encouragement, sympathy, and understanding to others.

The lighthouse

My Word is like the beacon of a lighthouse, shining in the darkness. You are like a sea captain piloting his ship on a dark sea. When you have no light, you cannot see the shoreline and your ship could be dashed against the rocks and lost.

But because I love you, I send out My Words like the huge beam of a lighthouse, sweeping the waters and seeking you out. My light shows you the dangers of the rocky shore and the way to a safe harbor. I built this lighthouse for you because I love you.

Look to My Word to get the light and guidance you need, so you can make it safely to port.

What is love?

Love is caring. Love is reaching out. Love is holding back words when appropriate. Love is taking a moment in a busy day to give someone a word of encouragement. Love is lending a helping hand, even when you are tired.

Love is Me—Jesus—and I am always there for you. Reach out when you need a hand, and I'll be there. I am there to help in whatever way you need it.

I love you with the kind of love that never quits or tires or gives up. You are My friend, and just as friends are there for each other, so am I there for you. Let Me be your closest friend and confidant, and I'll help you to grow in the knowledge of love, how it works, and how you can be My love to others.

Just as
My love
is present
in the
rainbow,
know that
it is also
there in the
raindrop of
affliction.

Do it for Me

There is really nothing that you could do that would last as long or accomplish as much real good as sharing Me and My love with others. And it's really not that hard, even if you've never made a conscious effort to do it before.

As you go for a walk or sit on a park bench, you can strike up a conversation and encourage and share My love with those you meet. You could even pass out tracts with messages about Me and My love and salvation.

If you have the energy for it, you could work as a volunteer at a homeless shelter, hospital, orphanage, church, or charity. Investing in others can rejuvenate your own body and spirit, as well.

So many others need My love. I would like to use your mouth, your hands, and your feet to carry My love to them. Be My hands and feet and heart and mouth. Let Me love others through you.

The best step

The last step of life—the one into My arms—will be the culmination of a long journey. That last step will be the *best* step. I will be there to greet you, embrace you, and welcome you to Heaven. Then we will experience total joy together. I so look forward to that moment!

ଓ

At your age, your body is just plain tired from the wear and tear of life. Your heart is tired from all the pumping, your muscles are tired from all the movement, your nerves are tired from all the strain, and on and on it goes. But if you didn't feel so tired and didn't have all the aches and pains you do, you wouldn't feel as much like leaving your old body behind and coming home to Heaven. This is one way I have of preparing you to move on.

You can't even imagine the wonderful things that await you in Heaven—best of all, the love. The love you will experience in Heaven is the purest and deepest and richest kind. This love is perfect in every way, and will make you feel more loved and more complete than you have ever felt before. It's like nothing you have ever known before. What a day that will be—rest from your labors, joy for your sorrows, recompense for your giving, and eternal bliss in My heavenly kingdom of love!

My quiet work

These are our quiet years together, My loved one, when I do a quiet work within you. These are the years when the strength of the flesh fades into the background so the strength of the spirit can flourish and grow. This is a special time for us to reflect and meditate—time that is no longer crowded out by former demands.

Having this special time to get closer to Me, your Creator, is not a punishment but a reward. While you may lament the tiredness and the weakening of your frame, I see beyond that and see the beauty of how your spirit is drawn closer to Me. As life slows down, I am able to speak to you more clearly. I want to answer your questions and heal your hurts. These times are part of My plan to prepare you for the next life.

Closer and closer

This is the reward for you who love Me: You will find that as the years pass, you will come closer and closer to Me. You will become sweeter and sweeter, and more and more loving. You will find more and more peace inside. Your spirit will be at rest.

You will find your soul drawing nearer to Heaven as you look ahead to the glories that await you here. And as you look toward the horizon, toward the blessing of knowing My love in its completeness in Heaven, know that I will always walk with you in this life. Then when the time comes, we will cross that river together, with Me holding your hand, until you step onto the golden shore that awaits you.

Oh, what a rejoicing there will be when we embrace on this side, in your heavenly dwelling place! You have many rewards waiting for you, and you will amass yet more rewards in the days before you come. That will be a glorious and beautiful day, but the days before you come will also be beautiful.

So rest in My arms, My dear friend, as we walk together day by day, closer and closer, until that final day when we walk no more apart but as close as breath to breath, and you know Me as intimately as I know you.

The journey

The road of life is long, with all its twists and turns, but I help you around every bend and over every mountain. Each step you take, each mile you travel, I go with you and watch over you.

You must walk this road a while longer, but the light you will encounter when you get to the end is going to be so warm, so beautiful, so all-encompassing, that you will realize that every step of the journey has been more than worth it. As I loved you before the world was made and as I love you now, I will love you then.

When this road ends and a new one begins, you will look at Me as an old and trusted friend and say, "I'm ready. Will You lead the way?" And I will.

I will always come to your rescue.
I may not always spare you from
problems, but I will pull you through
and give you faith to carry on. This
is the type of strength I want to show
others through you.

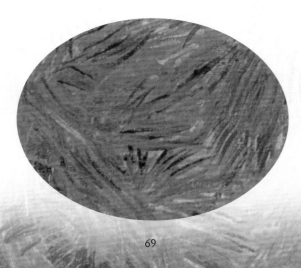

AFTERWORD

If you haven't yet experienced the kind of love expressed in these messages from Jesus, it may be that you haven't yet received His gifts of eternal love and life by accepting Him as your Savior. Jesus won't force Himself on you. He waits humbly for you to invite Him into your life. He says, "Behold, I stand at the door [of your heart] and knock. If anyone hears My voice and opens the door, I will come in" (Revelation 3:20). You can receive Him right now by sincerely praying the following:

Dear Jesus, thank You for dying for me, so I can have eternal life. Please forgive me now for every wrong and unloving thing I have ever done. Wash away all that, and help me to do better. I need Your love to fill and satisfy my heart. I want the life of heavenly happiness You have for me—here and now, and in Heaven hereafter. I open the door of my heart and ask You, Jesus, to come in. Thank You for hearing and answering my prayer. Amen.